Womanized

*A Dedication*

To anyone who's ever been or will ever be Womanized, anyone who knows someone who has been womanized, this book is written for you. Here's my attempt to give an understanding to those of you whose hearts have ever been affected by a guy like me. I dedicate this to you.

Sincerely, a womanizer

*Prologue*

Womanized

After witnessing what she had and crying herself to sleep, she figured she had enough evidence and had been through enough pain to call it quits. She picked up the phone and made the call.

"Hello?" he said.

"It's me," she said.

"I was just about to call you. We need to talk."

She was so drained from crying all morning that she couldn't even yell to show her real frustration. But she spoke firmly. "No. No we don't. I'm done talking. You've done me wrong. I've seen it with my own eyes. You've lied to, betrayed, and disrespected me. I don't see how we could go forward."

He didn't even bother to ask what she was talking about. "Me either," he said. "It's over." And he hung up.

Even though she'd called with the intention of breaking it off, that wasn't really what she wanted. She felt as if she'd lost—lost the best thing that had ever happened to her. Even though she felt he'd done her so wrong, she regretted making the phone call. He had a hold on her so strong that it seemed nothing or no one could break it. It was the same hold he'd had on just about every woman who'd ever entered his life—ever since he was a teen.

# Chapter 1 The Lesson After Class
## (Mama said)

Early Sunday morning, young Marques was awakened by his mother to get ready for their day at church with his grandmother. He was beat and didn't feel at all like going. He'd spent the whole night analyzing ways to beat the video game. But he rushed to get ready before his mom got angry. He rushed right out of the house looking like a slouch.

His mother stopped him in his tracks. "Where do you think you're going looking like that?"

"To church!" he said with a smirk. "It's all right. God said, 'Come as you are.'"

His mother smiled and said, "You are something else, but seriously, a man should always take pride in his appearance. I don't ever want to see you looking like you're not groomed and clean-cut. Now get in the car."

As he climbed into the backseat of the car, his grandmother said, "Why do you look so rough, boy? Anyone ever told you a man—"

"Should always take pride in his appearance?" said Marques. "Yes, I've heard that before. I think it was the beautiful love of my life who told me." He winked at his mother in the rear-view mirror, and she smiled back. "Speaking of beautiful, Grandma, you look amazing on this beautiful Sunday. Matter of fact, it's a blessing to be in your presence. I might as well just stay home and play the game, since I'm already blessed."

"Awwww, why, thank you," said his grandmother. "Now wipe that grin off your face and learn something today in Sunday school."

After spending the next three hours questioning everything his Sunday school teacher said, Marques met up with his mom in the car as his grandmother talked to the pastor. His mother asked, "What did you learn today?"

"I learned that women can't be trusted!"

"What?" said his mom.

"Yeah, women can't be trusted. I learned that Eve was naïve enough to be manipulated by a…" He laughed and then went on. "She was manipulated by a talking snake into disobeying God. If God can't trust her, who can?"

His mom, always honest and rather blunt with him, turned to him and said, "You're right. There's no way around it. Most women are naïve, easy to manipulate, and make decisions by emotion rather than logic, but I tell you what. You can always trust me. And trust me, this is not a conversation you want to keep going when your grandmother gets back in the car, so shut it up!"

# Chapter 2 Advised and advanced

## (Loraine)

This was one of many lessons Marques learned that summer.

Most of his summer was a blur, since he was rushing through it to get to his freshman year of high school. But he'd always vividly remember the night his hot, slightly older, gorgeous neighbor Loraine got into an argument with her boyfriend.

A woman shouting, "Get out!" drew Marques's attention to the house next door as he sat on his front stoop. It was Loraine. "Get out. Get out now!" she said to her boyfriend as he walked out to get in his car. "Maybe you should consider learning moves from the guys in all the porn you watch instead of masturbating to the women!"

Marques tried to hold it in but burst out laughing.

That drew Loraine's attention to him. She smirked, then strutted into her house.

Though he found it hilarious, he found it even more informative. So later that night, and from that point on, Marques took the advice an upset Loraine had given her embarrassed boyfriend. He studied every move the porn stars made, analyzing what it took to get certain types of moans and orgasms from the women.

One day when he was watching, as if he knew he'd soon use the moves as well as the old condom he carry everywhere with him, his mom called out frantically, "Marques! Come here!"

"OK! I'm on my way," he yelled back. He walked slowly, praying that he hadn't had the porn playing loud enough for her to hear. "Yes, ma'am?" he said, walking into the kitchen.

"Go over there and tell that little girl to turn that music down!" She was referring to eighteen-year-old Loraine, who was given the house for the summer by her uncle as a jump start to independence before she went off to be on her own at college.

"OK," said Marques. He checked himself in the mirror real quick, then headed over to Loraine's. He banged on the screen door, which he could see straight through. Loraine was dressed for bed and singing along to the loud stereo. He opened it when he saw she couldn't hear his knock and walked up on her.

When she saw him out of the corner of her eye, she screamed and jumped. "What are you doing in here?"

"I came to ask you to turn down the radio for my mom," he yelled over the loud music.

"Oh, I'm sorry. I didn't know it was that loud."

"It's all right, but are you?" he asked.

"Yes, I'm all right. Why do you think something's wrong?"

"Because you're blasting a song that says, 'I'm tired of these cold nights, pretending that it's all right.' But, hey, I could be wrong."

"Well, you're wrong. Nothing's wrong," said Loraine.

"Oh, OK. I would've thought you were lonely living out here away from your friends for the summer with no car. And you might be sexually frustrated from breaking up with your boyfriend, who wasn't pleasing you in the first place. But, hey, what do I know?"

With an astonished look on her face Loraine said, "You know too much."

Marques said, "I beg to differ. You can never know too much. I'm always open to learning. I try to learn something new every day, but I do know you're too attractive to be sexually frustrated."

"It's not all about looks, little boy"

"Well. I'm quite sure of that, but that's all I have to go on for now, but believe me, I definitely wouldn't mind stimulating you mentally, physically, emotionally, and spiritually. Well, maybe not emotionally, but everything else, sweetheart."

"Sweetheart? And why not emotionally?"

"I suffer from apathy. I've always lacked the ability to care for someone outside of family."

Blown away by his honesty and maturity, Loraine became more interested. "How old are you?"

"I just made fourteen this summer."

"Wow, you seem pretty advance for your age."

"I am—in more ways than you know."

After trying to pick Marques's brain and having it turned around on her in every way possible, a now turned on, lonely, horny, sexually frustrated Loraine found herself on her back on the couch with her panties pulled down. Young Marques had his face between her legs. He kissed her inner thighs and slowly dragged his tongue from her thighs to her clit. Then he began to suck and simultaneously lick before taking his two fingers and spreading the lips of her vagina. He licked in a circular motion, then moved both fingers in and out of her. When he moved his lips back to her clit and began sucking, he got his best reaction out of her yet. She started to shake, and she grabbed hold of his face as she moaned. He slipped that old condom out his back pocket and pulled himself up so that they were face to face. Then he started kissing her so she could taste herself.

He tried to insert himself into her, but she stopped him when she felt his size. "Wait," she said. "I have to get ready for you." She took a deep breath and slowly guided him into her.

He began moving rapidly, thinking back on the last scene he'd watched in the porn.

She whispered, "Slow down. Take your time. It's not going anywhere."

Once again, he took her advice and began to develop a rhythm. He started to observe what made her react the most. He found just the right spot, both on her neck, where his lips now lay, and inside of her, where he kept stroking as she wrapped her legs around him and dig her nails deeply into his back.

After orgasming, a selfish, drained, pleased, but confused Loraine said, "OK, we're done. Thanks. I'm sorry; I'll make sure you get yours next time."

Marques smirked. "It's OK. You're welcome."

He snuck back into his house past his now asleep mother and went into the basement to use the shower so he won't wake her. In the shower, he smiled to himself, adrenaline still pumping. Even though he hadn't ejaculated, he'd still gotten off. He was pleased with the fact that he had pleased Loraine and that she wanted there to be a next time. He also liked that she'd had to get ready for him after feeling his size. The thought of pleasing a woman was so powerful that he didn't even think about the fact that he'd just lost his virginity.

# Chapter 3 Understand, Control, Compromise

## (Loraine Part 2)

As the summer went on, even though he and Loraine had strong sexual encounters with each other, it had dawned on Loraine that there were certain things she liked that she couldn't do with a fourteen-year-old, like going to clubs. Still, she'd begun to lust for Marques and get advice from him.

Marques, for his part, could read Loraine and see that something was missing, so, lying in bed after sex one night, while sensually rubbing his fingers in her hair, he asked her what was wrong.

"Why does something always have to be wrong? Nothing's wrong. You were great."

Confident, Marques said, "I know I'm great. I wasn't talking about the sex though. You seem incomplete."

Loraine's smile disappeared. "You're right, I am incomplete, but I'm not sure I can talk to you about it."

"You can talk to me about anything. Just don't lie to me. I'm very understanding."

Loraine hesitated for a moment, but the she broke down and vented to him about how she wanted to do couple's activities but couldn't, because society wouldn't accept it. But she didn't think she could cut him off and completely and just be with her boyfriend, because her boyfriend didn't please her like Marques. "What's a girl to do? I'm so confused!" she said.

"Don't be. The solution is simple." He spoke as if he were the older of the two.

"It is?"

"Yes. Why can't you just do couple's activities with your boyfriend and let me continue pleasing you sexually?"

"Because I'll feel bad, that's why!"

"It's OK. I'll make you feel good every time."

"So you don't mind being used?"

"If being used means pleasing you, then no I don't mind."

"Why are you OK with this? Most guys wouldn't be this understanding."

"I'm not most guys. I'm very understanding. Didn't you hear me say that?"

Blown away, Loraine said, "This is just too much. I was taught you can't have your cake and eat it too."

"Well, who wants a cake they can't eat?" said Marques. "Sounds like a person who likes to be teased. I don't like being teased, do you?" Before she could answer, he added, "Matter of fact, I take that back. Come here." Still with his fingers in her hair, he firmly gripped the back of her head and instructed her where to kiss. He pointed to his neck. "Kiss here." Then he directed her to his chest. Then to his aroused penis. "And now here." He felt the warmth of her mouth on his penis as she looked up at him with her big, pretty eyes. Marques was in shock that this was happening, but he never let show on his face. In fact, he was replaying in his head all the unbelievable things that had gone on that summer while she stroked his shaft and licked around the head of his penis.

These thoughts were pleasing to Marques, but he had to admit that Loraine actually wasn't that great at giving fellatio. So he stood up and took control, doing something he saw in one of the many movies he'd watched that summer.

"Just hold your mouth open," he said. As he penetrated her mouth, she gagged and slapped him on the stomach. He smiles and started slowly stroking his penis in her mouth. Marques drifted off into thoughts about how it felt better now that he was in control. That thought would stick, and from that day on, he always liked to be in control of any situation involving him. He had more confidence in his abilities than anyone else's, so he wanted to be in control.

Soon, it was the end of the summer. Loraine called Marques over for a talk the night before she set off for college. She told him how great she'd felt since meeting him but that she understand they are both entering critical parts of their lives and were going to be meeting a lot of new people. She wanted him to take a vow that he'd wait on her while she was off at school and give her a chance to get him over being apathetic once she was back.

When she saw him staring back at her with a blank expression, Loraine realized she'd lost him with the request for a vow. "Marques, what do you think?"

"Loraine! I think a vow is a promise, and a promise is made to be broken, and I've been on the wrong end of broken promises. I'd rather not put myself in that situation."

"What? At your age, how many broken promises could you possibly have experienced?"

Marques was a rather guarded person when it came to his feelings. But that night, he opened up to Loraine. "One. One too many, when I was five years old and my parents split. My father vowed to pick me up every Saturday to spend the weekend at his place. Starting out, everything went as planned. Then it seemed as if every Saturday morning I was getting dressed to be lied to by a man who always taught me to be a man of my word. That was something I couldn't understand until my mom explained to me one day that situations change and things come up. She said I should refrain from being a liar. So to make sure I never fail to be a man of my word, I don't make promises, simply because things happen."

"Wow," she said. "I totally understand, but I want you to understand, and I know you should 'never say never,' but I'll never break a promise I make to you."

"Never say never is the biggest contradiction I've ever heard, but I guess all I have to go on is your word. Just don't lie to me. I hate liars. Lying is a sign of fear, and you have no reason to fear telling me the truth. I'm either going to understand or not care. Just don't lie to me. Understood?"

"Yes. Understood. I want you to give me a feeling that will last for these next four years."

"I rather give you a feeling that will last forever and a day," said Marques before having long, passionate, exotic sex with Loraine. And even though she enjoyed the multiple orgasms she'd had, there was still something bothering Loraine that she never brought up. She couldn't help but feel less of a woman for not being able to make the fourteen-year-old cum. This would be a thought Loraine took off to college with her and the subject of her vow.

*Chapter 4 MESSAGE!*

*( Mᶜ Butler )*

Between focusing on school work, extra after school classes he had picked up, and talking to Loraine every night on the phone, before Marques knew it, he looked up and found there were two weeks left in his senior year. And there was only one week left till his eighteenth birthday and prom, where he would finally reunite with Loraine, who was set to be his date.

Much as during all of high school, Marques was day dreaming about his plans after graduation. Then his reverie was broken.

"Marques! Marques Thomas," said his twenty-six-year-old English teacher, Ms. Butler.

To Marques, she looked much like the porn star who played the role of a teacher in one of the movies he'd seen. "Yes, Ms. Butler?"

"I need a word with you after class."

As the bell rang and everyone exited the class, Ms. Butler was sitting on the corner of her desk. Marques approached her and sat on the opposite side of the desk, planning to stall so he wouldn't have to go to his next class.

"What's up?" he said. "You wanted to tell me how I had the best final project you've ever seen?"

"It is, Mr. Arrogant, but that's not what I wanted."

"Well, what's up? I can tell something's bothering you."

"Nothing. Well, I do wish some of your classmates would get it together. There are only two weeks left. I mean, what's the use of having a brain if you won't use it?"

"Oh, so you wanted tips on how to run the class? It's a little too late for that now, don't you think?"

"No, smart aleck, I wanted to know if you'd like to take Sharon Taylor to the prom. She asked me if I could talk to you."

"No," said Marques abruptly.

"Why not? She's sweet, smart, and has tons of potential."

"You should be her prom date, then."

"What's up with you? I've seen you dodge and turn down girls all year. I know you're focused on school, but come on. You're still a young man. You're at an age when your hormones are raging. You're smart, charming, have a sense of humor, are always well-groomed—"

"Handsome."

"Yes, handsome. You're handsome also, Marques."

"Thanks," said Marques with a smirk. "You're not too bad-looking yourself. But seriously, there's someone I made a vow to who'll be coming home from school to accompany me to the prom. My loyalties lie with her."

"Humph! Loyalty."

"What does that mean? I knew there was something wrong."

"No. It's just my friend."

"Boyfriend?"

"No. She's a friend from college who promised she'd visit for the summer. Then backed out at the last minute because she's reunited with her high school sweetheart. It's already bad enough, I was going to have to share her with this mystery man she's been babbling about since I took her under my wing in my senior year when she was just a freshman. She says he's the guy who gave her a feeling that 'lasts a day and forever,' but now that she's reunited with this guy from high school, I can barely get in contact with her. I have to change my whole summer plans. Why am I telling you this. Isn't there somewhere you should be?"

"Oh, so you're upset that she has two boyfriends and you don't have one?"

"I'm not upset. Just disappointed. And, for the record, if you must know, I do have a boyfriend."

"But?"

She laughed. "But he's just too sweet. He lets me have my way. No woman wants a guy she can run over."

"Makes sense. But if he was too strict, you'd feel the need to rebel, no?"

"Yes, I just need a guy who knows how to balance it all out. A guy that's—"

"Like a good father? Give you your way, let you be daddy's girl and spoil you, but also knows when to put you in your place and not let you run wild?"

Astonished, Ms. Butler said, "Yes, a guy like that is what I need!"

"Well, why not leave the guy you're with and find a guy like that?"

"Because I love him, that's why. You don't just leave someone you love."

"So stay with someone you're unhappy with because you love him? That has zero logic to it."

"You have to understand, women are emotional creatures. We don't need logic; we have feelings."

"What's the use of having a brain if you won't use it? Mind over heart. Being in a situation that makes you unhappy doesn't mean you're in love, it means love has made you stupid."

Ms. Butler tried hard not to let it show that everything the seventeen-year-old had said struck a chord with her. "Stupid is as stupid does," she said. Now take this pass and go to your fourth period class."

Leaving with a smirk and fifteen minutes left in his fourth period class, Marques learned a couple of extra lessons of his own after class.

The weekend passed without Marques hearing from Loraine for the first time since she'd been off at school. Something wasn't right, so he called—and called and called, with no answer. So he tried a text before school Monday. "Hey, Loraine, is everything all right? Are you OK?"

Marques spent the first two periods of school thinking about what he'd do about prom if Loraine didn't show. He would still have to go. It would break his mother heart and pocket book if he cancelled last minute.

While walking to Ms. Butler's class, he got a text back from Loraine's phone. "Yeah, everything's all right. She's great."

"Who's this?" Marques texted back."This is her boyfriend. Who's this?" Marques read the text, and then he deleted the thread of messages.

# Chapter 5 Prom Night
## (Goodbye M<sup>c</sup> Butler, Hello Melissa)

"Hey, Ms. Butler. I need to talk to you after class," he said as he walked into the classroom.

When class ended, he approached Ms. Butler in a sort of shameful manner. "Does Sharon still need a date for the prom," he said. "Or did you decide to take my advice and take her?"

Ms. Butler laughed. "No, funny guy, she actually accepted an invitation from someone else after I told her you said no. Why do you ask?"

"Didn't want to break all the girls' hearts walking in there by myself."

"By yourself? What happened to your college girl?"

"I flirted with the thin line between loyalty and stupidity and ended up on the wrong side."

"Yeah, you can miss out on a lot of opportunities waiting with or on the wrong person. Choose who you spend your time with wisely, because it's the only thing in life you can't get back. But, hey, you'll be all right."

"Yeah, I'm always all right."

"You won't be the only one flying solo that night though. I'm chaperoning alone. I broke up with my boyfriend."

Marques sarcastically said, "How could you just break up with someone you love like that?"

"Mind over heart!" said Ms. Butler with a laugh. "The situation was stressing me. I need a massage. I'm playing everything safe. I even carry a condom in my purse now." She smiled.

"Really?"

Ms. Butler quickly switched subjects. "Come around the desk and tell me what you think of this dress. I may wear it to the prom."

"I like it. It looks like something Loraine wore in a picture she sent to me."

"Loraine?"

"Yeah, Loraine, my ex-prom date."

"Oh! The college girl. What college was it that she went to again?"

"FAMU."

"Oh, cool. Great school. Why was it again she canceled on you?"

"Because apparently she broke our vow and got a boyfriend."

"You don't seem that disappointed."

"I'm not. I learned at a young age that women can't be trusted, but enough about her, more about you and your dress."

"Yes. The dress. Is it a no or yes?"

"Yes!"

"Good. I think you have great taste."

"And I think you taste great!"

Before she knew it, Ms. Butler found herself relaxed in her chair behind her desk with her panties pulled down. Marques was under the desk with his face between her legs. He kissed her inner thighs and slowly dragged his tongue from her thighs to her clit. He then began to suck and simultaneously lick before taking his two fingers and spreading the lips of her vagina and licking in a circular motion. Then he began to work both fingers in and out of her while taking the focus of his lips back to her clit and sucking. He got his best reaction out of her yet. She started to shake and grab hold of his face as she moaned. He slipped that condom out of her purse and pulled himself up. Face to face, he kissed her so she could taste herself. Then he turned her around and bent her over the desk. He tried to insert himself in her from the back.

But she stopped him when she felt his size. "Wait," she said. "I have to get ready for you." She cleared the desk while propping her upper body and one leg on top of it. Then she looked back at him, slowly guiding him into her. He began easing himself in and out of her slowly.

"Go faster," she whispered. "Fuck me harder! We can't be forever. We can't get caught."

He began to develop a rhythm and to observe what made her react the most. He found her spot inside of her, one hand on her waist and the other on the back of her neck. He pound her repeatedly, stroking hard as she dug her nails deeply into the papers remaining on the desk. Reaching orgasm, she yelled to him, "Tell me it's good!"

"It's good!"

"Tell me, 'It's good, Ms. Butler!'"

"It's good Ms. Butler! Ms. Butler! Ms. Butler!" said Marques as he walks back into the classroom and saw a zoned out yet relaxed Ms. Butler at her desk.

"What?" said Ms. Butler, startled at his entry.

"I left my book on your desk."

She looked a bit bashful and slightly embarrassed. "Here, take it now and run to class, boy." She realized she'd day dreamed of having sex with the young Marques immediately after he'd left for his next class after giving her advice on her dress.

After spending the week making last-minute preparations for prom, the day had finally come. Marques had turned eighteen and was getting ready to set off to prom.

As she straighten his tie, Marques's mother asked "How does it feel?"

"A little too tight around the neck, Mom."

"No, silly. I'm talking about it being your birthday! How does it feel to be eighteen?"

"Oh. No different from seventeen. How do I look?"

"Is that really a question? You're as handsome as ever. Remember to take a lot of pictures."

"Thanks. You're the reason, and OK, will do. See you later."

Marques pulls up to the banquet hall and walked in like he was the president of the United States, confident as ever, head high, skin as smooth and clear as a baby's, a smile that seemed as if it was the reason the room was lit so brightly.

"Hey there, handsome. Happy birthday!" said Ms. Butler as she almost snuck up on him.

"Hey, thanks a lot, gorgeous," said Marques with a grin.

"How old do you make today? Twelve?" she said, bending this way and that in an exaggerated inspection of Marques's baby face.

"No, I made the same age as you today. Eighteen."

"Oh don't make me blush!" she said.

Then they went their separate ways and to enjoy the night's festivities. As the night was about to end and it was time for the final dance, Marques spotted Ms. Butler over near the buffet, where she sat and monitored the room while sipping wine all night.

He walked over to her. "May I?"

"May you what? You're too young."

"No, I'm not. We're the same age, remember? Plus, it's just one dance."

She laughed. "OK, come on. And you better not try anything."

"OK, I won't if you won't."

Between having one too many glasses of wine and Marques rubbing too close to her in his tailored tux, Ms. Butler begins to get hot and bothered. "Woooo! Yeah, it's time for me to call my cab," she said. "Hope you enjoyed your birthday and prom."

"Cab? No. I won't allow it, he said with a laugh. I have an empty passenger seat for you. I'll take you."

"No. How would that look? Me leaving with my student?"

"You're right. We can wait till everyone leave. Besides, I'm only dropping you off."

"OK, fine. I'll allow it."

When they arrived at her apartment, Marques asked Ms. Butler if he could come up and get a little rest before his drive home. "Safety first. I made sure you got home safe. Now let's be sure I get there the same way."

"OK, you rest up while I take a shower and get ready for bed."

After a thirty-minute shower, she reappear from the bathroom in nothing but a leopard print underwear set. "You're still here?"

"Yeah, I was waiting to give you that massage you said you needed earlier this week."

"Oh, pahlease!"

"No need to beg. I'm offering," said Marques. He walked in close on Ms. Butler and kissed her. She didn't resist at all. In fact, she reacted to Marques sticking his tongue in her mouth in a way that would make someone think he was the man of her dreams, getting her aroused, her face all ablaze with excitement.

Marques guides her back into the door. As it swung open, a bed came into view. He pushed her onto the bed and climb on top of her.

"What are you doing?"

"Shhhh. You're asking too many questions," said Marques as he began to kiss her. He tried to insert himself, only to be stopped.

"No! Like this," said Ms. Butler. She bent over to the doggy-style position and began to push herself back onto him. Marques grabbed her waist to get a grip, and she instantly started to yell out instructions. "Fuck me! Fuck me! Fast! Harder!"

Feeling controlled, Marques did as she said, but he took control by gripping the back of her neck and turning her face to look back at him as he fucked her harder. The look on her face was one of astonishment yet pleasure. The harder he went, the farther up the bed she scooted, until he had her pinned in a corner up against the wall.

She whispered, "I knew you had some good sex. Slap my ass. Please slap my ass." Marques proceeded to follow her orders but also pulled her hair. "Oh my god! said Ms. Butler. "We have to stop. You're giving me a feeling that I shouldn't be having."

Increasing the pace of his stroke, Marques whispered, "Are you sure?"

"No," she whispered.

He went deeper. "You sure?"

"OK, break time!"

Ms. Butler instantly went to sleep, while Marques sat up in the bed and thought a little before falling asleep. The next morning, he awoke to her sitting up over him looking at him, caressing him.

He looked at her and smiled. "What's up?"

"Did you enjoy yourself last night?"

"Yeah, prom was all right. It's kind of overrated."

"Not talking about prom, silly. I mean with me."

"Yeah, I did." Looking at the dried up puddle on her side of the bed, he smirked. "No need to ask you the same question."

"Why do you last so long?"

"So long? You wanted a break after about forty minutes."

"Yeah, I know. Most guys, at best, only last fifteen minutes."

"Well, I'm not most guys. How did you know?"

"Know what?"

"That I had good sex? Last night you said, 'I knew you had some good sex.'"

"Oh. It was just those glasses of wine talking."

"Drunken words are sober thoughts. So you thought about it before?"

"OK. You got me. I have a confession," she said.

"I'm listening."

"Loraine," she said.

"What about her?"

"Loraine was my friend from college who cancelled on me. I figured it out once you said her name and told me she went to my alma mater. I couldn't help but think about all the stories she told me about you. I even daydreamed about how she told me your very first time was together—in my classroom that day."

"Forever and a day," said Marques.

"What?" she said, looking confused.

"Forever and a day. It's 'forever and a day' not 'a day and forever,' like you said when you were telling me the feeling your roommate said her mystery man gave her. I knew Loraine was your roommate from that point."

"Wow!" she said, shocked. "So you knew all this time and didn't care?"

"No. Why should I?"

"Your loyalty to her. What happened to it?"

"It didn't exist once she broke our vow and we weren't communicating anymore. Without communication you're bound to end up not being on the same page, and if you're not on the same page, someone will finish that book before you can. But enough about her. I'd rather not speak about her."

"OK, sir. I'd rather speak about last night anyway."

"What about it?"

"Don't you want to know if I thought you were good or not?"

He looked down at the spot on the sheets again and then back up at her. "It's evident."

"Oh, OK, Mr. Confident. You were great, but it isn't as evident for me, so I have to ask."

"Oh, you were great too."

"I couldn't tell. You didn't even cum."

"That had nothing to do with you. Plus, we didn't use protection. Where do you suggest I should have cum, Ms. Butler?"

"In me, Marques. Don't be silly, and call me Melissa."

"OK, don't be silly, Melissa," said Marques, who had begun to get dressed rapidly because he was uncomfortable with Melissa's statement. "I have to go home now. See you later."

# Chapter 6 Selfish
## (Melissa)

Marques arrived home to his mom, who seemed rather sad.

"Hey, gorgeous. What's wrong?"

"We have to talk," she said. "Come here and sit down."

After hearing the news from his mom, Marques felt lost. He was overcome with so much emotion that he didn't even notice that he was becoming withdrawn over the next week.

His mom told him, "It's all right. It's going to be OK. It's life."

But Marques could see through her forced positivity and see that "life" had gotten to her. He noticed she was hiding her pain over the whole situation.

The week had past and so had graduation, when Marques, restless but extremely tired from not sleeping for days, got a call one afternoon from what seemed to be a concerned Melissa, who bombarded him with questions.

"Hey! How are you? Why haven't I heard from you? Why were you not at graduation? Is something wrong?"

Before Marques could say anything, she continued.

"When can I see you? Can you come over today? I want to see you."

Marques decided to go over to take his mind off the past week.

"Sure. I'll be on my way."

An eager Melissa sat in the window waiting for Marques. She buzzed him in before he could ring the doorbell. When he walked in the door, he saw that she was partially nude and rushing toward him.

"I missed you," Melissa said excitedly as she kissed his cheeks. She wrap one hand around his neck and stroke his penis with her other hand. She led him to the bedroom and pulled him down onto the bed on top of her. They began passionately going at it. Marques, still aroused, abruptly stopped and roll off of her. He had begun to think about the events of the past week. Upset, Melissa stormed out the room and into the shower. Marques followed about five minutes later only to find Melissa weeping in the shower.

"Hey, what's wrong? Why are you crying? Stop crying."

"No, I won't! You're selfish. You've made me want you then blocked me out for a week. And now you just stop in the middle of sexing me? Don't ever do that. It's not right."

"I couldn't continue. I have a lot on my mind. My grandmother past the last time I was with you. We buried her the morning of graduation. It took a lot out of me. I haven't slept in days. I almost became asthmatic at the funeral. I was crying and couldn't stop wheezing. I just couldn't see her lying there like that. That's why I stopped. I'm drained."

"Aw, baby, I'm sorry to hear that." She grabbed the back of his head.

"It's OK. You don't have to be sorry, just respect how I'm feeling at the moment. I appreciate it."

"OK, I will, baby. Go in there and get you some sleep."

Marques did just that. Knackered from the sleepless week, he fell into an almost coma-like sleep only to wake about fifteen minutes later to what sounded like Melissa saying, "You're going to cum in me." She was giving him fellatio in a way that seemed not to please him but to get him aroused enough for her to climb on top of his exhausted body and rapidly start moving back and forth. She put her arm under his back and forced him upward inside of her while he lay helpless until they both simultaneously climaxed. Melissa then rolled off of Marques and into a slumber of her own with a smile on her face.

He woke the next day to the smell of breakfast and the deep thoughts of how Melissa had selfishly disregarded his feelings to satisfy herself. And he'd let himself become so physically and emotionally drained that he couldn't do anything. More importantly, she may have been impregnated, and he couldn't and wouldn't want to imagine himself having a child with her.

Angry, he called her into the room. "Melissa, get in here. Now!

"Yes, baby."

"Don't call me that. And don't lie to me. Are you on birth control?"

# Chapter 7 All Figured Out
## (Melissa Part 2)

Looking slightly amused Melissa sipped her iced tea and smiled. "Of course I am, silly. Don't worry."

Marques didn't entirely believe her. "Why shouldn't I worry? I'm not ready for children and not really sure if I want any—ever."

The comment seemed abrupt and absurd to Melissa. "Oh, wow! Get married, have children, live happily. That's how it's supposed to go. How are you going to say you're not sure if you ever want children?"

"How are you going to tell me what I'm 'supposed' to do?" he yelled. "Don't say 'supposed' to me. I despise the word. How could anyone set guidelines for another person to follow in life without knowing what works for that person just because it has worked for them? Those guidelines could potentially be setting a person up for failure."

"Wow! You're absolutely right. I stand corrected. I can't wait to see how far your mind goes after college."

"College? Who said I was going to college?"

"You're not going to college? You have to go to college. You're supposed to go to college."

"What did I just tell you about that word?"

"I apologize. But why are you not going to college?"

"Because I feel it's not for everyone, and I feel I'll be misusing my time if I spend the next four years in someone's college."

"Oh, OK. So what are you going to spend the next four years doing?"

"Investing the money my grandmother left me when she passed."

Melissa was intrigued. "Oh? And how much did she leave you?"

Marques stiffened a bit. "Enough. She left me enough. Now, any more questions, or can we eat breakfast before it gets too cold?"

"No, no more questions. I apologize if I offended you. Let me make it up to you." Melissa, dressed in a very attractive cherry red underwear set, dropped to her knees. She took a piece of ice from her tea and put it in her mouth. Then she wrapped her lips around his penis and squeezed tight as pliers as she slowly went back and forth, giving him the pleasure of feeling the coldness of the ice and warmness of her mouth. She rolled her tongue and the ice around the head of his penis then sped up, as if the tease was over and she was ready to receive the ultimate reward of Marques's warm cum in her mouth. She worked both hands on his penis while still sucking and slobbering all over it. The more Marques reacted, the more aggressive she got. It was turning her on to please him. He noticed her juices running down her leg in a stream. Then he grabbed the back of her head and began thrusting into her mouth, telling her to not stop sucking. When he couldn't hold back any longer, he came in her mouth, moving his legs on the bed as if he were back pedaling. She sucked the cum out of him and swallowed it down. Marques seemed pleased and well over the earlier unpleasant conversation. Partially because he had imagined that it was the attractive saleswoman Katherine at the department store that shot down his advances when he went to purchase something to wear to his grandmother's funeral but mainly because what Melissa had figured out.

Melissa had figured out the one thing he was yet to gain control over within himself, which was his addiction to sex. Over the summer this became her method of distracting him from any problem that could potentially have led to him ending things between the two of them, from the middle-of-the-night accusatory voice mails to the randomly popping up at his mother's house with the hopes of catching him with someone else. Melissa figured it would be no different when the day came for her to propose something to him that had been on her mind the whole summer.

After a bout of intense, passionate sex on a breezy summer night, she felt the time was perfect. She looked over at a relaxed Marques. "Hey, what do you think about me quitting my job?"

"I think you should do whatever makes you happy."

"Good, because I've decided not to go back this school year."

"Oh? So what are you going to do about your rent and bills?"

"Well, I figured since you're not going off to college, you moving in would be a great idea. We could build with each other."

"Build with each other? We have sex. We please each other. That's as far as it could be built. I don't want anything more than that. Me moving in with you and paying your rent and bills is a terrible idea, no matter how you put it."

"Aw, baby, don't get so worked up. We'll talk about it tomorrow." Melissa reached over and begin stroking his penis.

"Yeah, let's just let our bodies talk right now," said Marques as he climbed on top of her and began wildly stroking her insides like a beast, going deeper than his thoughts while she clawed his back like she was clawing for life but nonetheless enjoying every moment of it. Then she pushed him off of her as she climaxed, squirting onto the sheets.

She smiled up at him. "Thank you, Marques."

She quickly fell asleep. But Marques spent the next thirty minutes thinking about the different crazy encounters he'd had with Melissa over the summer. Then he reflected on the conversation they had prior to the last time they had sex. He eased out the bed, got dressed, and left her there sleeping, vowing to sever all ties with her.

Forty-five minutes after arriving home, Marques received a text. It said, "Hey, I apologize for the way I've treated you over the summer, but I really need someone to talk to right now. I don't feel like living. Can you meet me?"

Caught off guard, Marques texted back. "Sure, don't do anything crazy. Where are you?"

# Chapter 8 WildKat
## (Katherine)

Marques arrived at the meeting spot and saw her sitting in her car, bruised and battered, eyes overflowing with tears.

"Katherine, what happened? Who did this to you?" he asked.

Katherine was embarrassed to say who was responsible for her current state, given the fact that it was the same person she blew off Marques for all summer, the same person who had her scared to accept Marques phone number the first day he saw her standing in the clothing store with a beautiful smile that he could see was hiding what seemed to be more pain and hurt than her small frame could handle. "My boyfriend," she finally said. "My boyfriend of five years. He got angry that I went out with my friends, and he began to beat me. I love him so much. I don't understand why he did this, and I couldn't call my friends, because they're all judgmental and think I should leave him. I don't want to be judged." She was crying harder now.

"No judgment will be passed," said Marques. "That's not why I'm here." He slid into the passenger seat of her car.

"I just feel so stupid. No matter how many times he does this, I always go back. I know he has a good heart. I just love him so much, but I guess love really is pain."

"No, love is what you make it. It doesn't have to be painful. I don't know your complete situation, but these bruises shouldn't be covering your beauty."

"I thought you said no judgment would be passed. He loves and cares for me so much that he just wants to protect me. He just has a different way of expressing it when I disobey what he feels is right, but his intentions are always good."

"I'm not judging," said Marques. "Like I said, it's not why I came here, and I definitely didn't come here to bad-mouth your boyfriend. As a matter of fact, let's talk less about him and more about you, beautiful."

"You've called me beautiful twice already, even though I'm beat up and looking ugly right now." Katherine laughed lightly. "That's more than I've heard all year. I rarely get complimented at home. Thanks a lot."

"No problem. I'm only stating facts. Don't call yourself ugly." Marques noticed Katherine's self- esteem was low.

"You seem like a great guy. What does your girlfriend think about you giving your number to strangers and meeting up with them at the wee hours of the morning while they're beat up and vulnerable?"

"I don't have a girlfriend," said Marques.

"It's OK. You don't have to lie to me. I'm pretty sure you have one."

"First you were beat up and ugly. Now you're *pretty* sure. Make up your mind." Marques and Katherine chuckled together. "How could you be so sure, anyway?" he said.

"I mean, you're handsome, well-groomed, seem to have a way with words, and you have a sense of humor. Someone has to have taken you off the market."

"Thanks, but no relationship for me. I don't want to be in one. I'm not the relationship type. It's very hard for me to have feelings for someone outside of family, let alone trust them. When you're in a relationship you're basically trusting a person to not disrespect, mistreat, or betray you, and I'm not sure if I can trust a person not to do those things, but I know for sure I won't do them to myself. Plus, I feel that if you're in a relationship with someone, it should be someone you plan on marrying and spending the rest of your life with, otherwise you're wasting your time and limiting yourself."

They wound up talking until daylight broke. This would become one of many long conversations between the two over the next few weeks, drawing Katherine close to Marques. He did the exact opposite of her boyfriend, Anthony, making her feel confident, wanted, and free to speak and act without being judged. She loved it and wanted to show him how much she appreciated it after work on a special day.

"Hey, Marques, can you pick me up from work today?"

"Sure, but where's your car?" asked Marques.

"My boyfriend locked it in the garage so I wouldn't be able to get around while he's gone."

"Oh, OK. You're not concerned with him seeing you in the car with another guy?"

"No. He's in Amsterdam with his brothers for his birthday, so please pick me up at two o'clock, and I can give you my housewarming gift and hopefully see how your new bachelor pad looks."

As he pulled up to pick up Katherine, he checked his texts and saw a simple "Hey" from Melissa. Having ignored her for weeks, Marques decided to reply. After all, the greeting was a major step forward from her recent threats and accusations.

"Hey, what's up?" he replied to Melissa as Katherine got into the car.

Melissa replied, "Can we have sex?"

He quickly texted, "No."

"No texting while driving, Marques. It's dangerous!" said Katherine.

"OK. Let me just respond to this last one." He looked around, making sure he was driving safely. Then he read the incoming text from Melissa, which said, "Take her home, Marques!"

"You know what?" said Marques to Katherine. "You're right. No texting while driving. I need to be focused. There are a lot of crazy people out here." He put his phone down without replying to the text.

When they entered Marques's apartment, Katherine looked around and nodded in approval. "Show me your bedroom," she said. He dropped his keys on the living room table, just as he always did, and then led her through the bedroom door. "It's right in here," he said.

Katherine blew past him, dropped the sheet set she'd bought him as a house warming gift, and flopped onto his bed.

"Come here. Don't be shy," she said in a tempting voice.

"I'm not shy, just aware."

"Aware of what?" she asked.

"My charming personality and sexual capabilities. I let you get the experience of one already. If you get both, dangerous things might happen, like you falling in love." Marques smirked, although he was extremely serious.

"You do have a great personality, but don't flatter yourself, and don't brag. People who brag are the ones who aren't that good at—" Katherine sat up in bed with a start as her phone rang. She looked at the caller ID. "Shh," she said, putting her finger to her lips.

"It's my boyfriend. Please don't say anything. He'll kill me if he hears another man's voice." There was fear in her voice.

"Don't worry. I won't, but you might want to hurry and answer before he gets suspicious."

"Hello?" she said into the phone. "Hey, honey, happy birthday!"

"Yeah, yeah," said her boyfriend angrily. Where are you? Why did it take so long to answer your phone? Who are you with?"

"I'm not with anyone. I'm at home."

Marques looks at her and pantomimes taking a shower.

"I was in the shower," Katherine shook her head in frustration but smirked at Marques.

"Why don't I believe you?" her boyfriend asked.

"You never believe anything I say!" Katherine yelled.

That sparked a heated argument between the two. As Marques watched silently, Katherine's face turned red, and tears rolled down her cheeks. Marques sat down beside her and began running his hand up her skirt while kissing her neck. He put his lips to her ear and whispered, "Calm down. Tell him that you're sorry for raising your voice, and it won't happen again."

Aroused, Katherine did exactly that. Then she grabbed the back of Marques's head as he continued kissing, sucking, and licking her neck in a way that had her mind racing. She imagined him using his soft lips and extremely long tongue for cunnilingus. He pushed her back and climbed on top of her.

Katherine asked her boyfriend how his trip was going and whether he was having fun.

Marques unbuttoned her blouse and softly kissed her breast, then her stomach. He slowly stroked her breast while and unzipping her skirt with his teeth.

"You're asking too many questions," said her boyfriend. "I'll talk to you later."

Katherine ended the call, tossed the phone aside, and challenged Marques by finishing her initial statement in a soft but daring voice: "Like I was saying, people who brag are the ones who aren't that good!"

Marques pulled himself back up and dragged his tongue from her now exposed breast to her neck. He began sucking, then he whispered in her ear, "I'll let my actions speak louder than my words, and I'll let your moans speak louder than my actions." He slowly inserted himself into her, then set about to please her in every way she could had imagined.

"Wow," she said. "He's never done that before!" She didn't notice that all Marques had done was remember all the sexual things she'd told him she liked during one of their long conversations: her favorite position, pulling her hair, moaning in her ear in a manly way. "Woooo! Oh, my God. My legs can't stop shaking."

He smiled. "You're welcome." After showering for about fifteen minutes, he laid down to take what was meant to be a quick nap. It turned out to be three hours long. He was awakened by her when she cuddled up to him and wrapped her arms around him.

"How long have you been awake?" he said. "Are you ready to go home now?"

"Oh, not long, and I'm not, but I have work in the morning. So, yeah, I guess we could leave."

As they were getting ready to leave, he noticed his keys were not on the table. "Hey, did you see where I set my keys?" he said.

Turning to the key hooks by the front door, Katherine grabbed the keys. "Yeah, they're right here on the key hook, where everyone puts their keys, silly."

On the ride home, Kat brought up the topic of leaving her boyfriend and being with Marques. "What do you think?" she asked.

"What do I think? I think if you're going to leave him, do it because you want to, not because of me."

"I do want to, and I'm going to, so what do you think about me being with you?

"I think I told you I wasn't the relationship type," he said in a stern manner.

"Oh, but I'm certain I can change that." She sounded confident.

"You can try."

And trying is just what Katherine did. She tried so much that she started to believe they were an item. In his nonchalance, Marques didn't notice until the day they were out at the grocery store and they saw Danielle Johnson, an upperclassman from when he was in high school.

"Hey, what's up, Danielle?" Marques said with a smile while Katherine looked on.

"Oh, wow, hey!" said Danielle. "Funny running into you congratulations!"

Confused, Marques said, "Thanks, but for what?"

"For moving into your new apartment.I was just at the school getting some advice from Ms. Butler on teaching children, and she said you all kept in touch after you graduated. She said she'd stopped by your place the other day to give you a housewarming gift, but you missed her call. She also told me she thought you'd be great to talk to the young men at the boys and girls club I'm starting so that I can keep busy while my husband's at work."

"Oh, yeah. Thanks again. That'll be great. Take my number, and just let me know all of the details." He gave the cashier enough money to cover his and her groceries, upsetting Katherine more than he could have even imagined. On the ride back to Marques's place, Katherine, who was driving, calmly asked, "Why didn't you introduce me?"

"Didn't feel the need to. It was just a hi-and-bye kind of thing."

"Didn't feel the need to?" she yelled. "I'm your girlfriend. Why wouldn't you feel the need to?"

"First of all, lower your tone when you're talking to me. Secondly, you're not my girlfriend. Thirdly, there is no thirdly, just remember not to raise your voice at me and that we're not a couple."

"We're not a couple? Oh, yes we are. We'll discuss that later, but for now, why did you pay for her groceries? Bob Evans, Oscar Meyer, Simply Orange, Voss! Voss!"

Marques chuckled, thinking it was funny that she'd remembered all the brand names. "It was just a nice gesture, Katherine."

She pulled into the apartment complex. "It's not funny. Get the groceries out so we can go upstairs and discuss this."

As Marques reached in through the back door of the car to get the bags of groceries, Katherine pulled off slowly, coming close to dragging Marques. He jumped back out of the way just in time.

As he walked into his apartment, he sent a text Katherine. "You're crazy," it said. "Never come near me again."

"I'll be near you all I want," she texted back. "As long as I'm carrying your child. I'm three weeks pregnant, and it's yours. I haven't been with anyone else." She attached a picture of a pregnancy test that read positive.

# Chapter 9 Keys and Pregnancies
## (Katherine Part 2: Lesson Learned)

Marques decided not to reply to the text, knowing that he'd always used protection when having sex with her.

But after days of thinking about it, he remembered the one time the condom had broken. So he did text her. "We need to talk about the baby," he said. Marques left his phone in the bedroom to go into the kitchen and check on the food he'd been cooking. When he returned to the room, he saw that he'd missed Katherine's call and that she had left a voice mail. Before calling her back, he decided to check the voice mail. It wasn't from Katherine. The voice was that of an angry, hostile male. "Don't text my woman's phone!" he said. "There is no baby. I made her have an abortion. I didn't want a baby by a cheating whore. Saturday would have made four weeks since I got her pregnant, but she don't deserve my baby."

Marques deleted the message, but he received twelve more, all from Katherine's phone. The last one was followed by a text: "I'm so sorry. Answer the phone. It's me. I needed someone to talk to when you weren't replying to my messages so I called him. I swear I'm not with him. Answer the phone, please, Marques."

He texted her back, "No. And I don't care. That's not my business. Lose my number." He ate dinner and went to sleep.

While in a deep sleep, he feels something dripping on his face. It woke him with a start. When he opened his eyes, he saw Katherine sitting over him and crying.

"How did you get in my house?" he asked calmly.

"I'm sorry. I love you. Please forgive me," said Katherine.

Now he raised his voice. "Shut up. How did you get in here?"

"Please don't be mad at me."

"I won't. Now how did you get in here? I don't want to ask again."

"The first day I was here, I took your keys off the table and went and got a set made. Please don't be mad."

"You're crazy!" said Marques. "Give me the keys, now."

"OK, here. Just don't call me crazy. I'm not crazy. I just—I just—you don't know what I've been through. I love you, but you've made it clear you don't love me back. You won't even introduce me as your girlfriend when we're out. So what else am I supposed to do besides go back to what I know in Anthony? But when I went back to him, nothing had changed. He said he wanted to have a baby with me and build a family, but all he did was bring down my self-esteem. He made it seem like there was no one else out there better than him, and the next guy would treat me the same way he did. So when you rejected me, as great as you are, I believed him. He made me feel low as a woman. Every bruise made me love myself less. And how could I respect myself if I allowed it? He wanted to control my mind, the way I act around people, the way I talk to him…he wanted me to change myself for his family. I stayed because I love him. And I love you too, but as hard as he is on me physically I felt I had a better chance of changing him than I do you. But the abuse just continued, and it got worse after we found out I was pregnant. I knew for a fact there was no changing him, so that's why I told you the baby was yours—in hopes of changing your mind and persuading you to build a family with me. He told me as long as I was carrying his child, he owned me like I was some type of property. Right then and there, I had to choose between my life and my baby's life. So after you didn't respond to my text, I knew what I had to do. I can't allow him to own me. Earlier today, he saw my text messages to you, and it hurt him to see you had a different type of hold on me, so we got into a real bad fight, and he had me by my neck, throwing me against the wall, choking me. Then he pushed me down and even spit in my face. I told him I wished he was dead, and it seemed to get to him. So he stormed out of the house, came back drunk, and then passed out. I took the opportunity to sneak over here. Please don't make me go back, please. We can never talk anything out. He won't allow me to speak. He treats me like I'm beneath him." Tears continued to roll down Katherine's face.

"I hate for you to have to go through something like that," said Marques. "It's horrible. I don't want to see you go back there, but you can't stay here either. I don't trust you. You're a liar. You should have told me the truth from the beginning."

"I know, I know, but the truth hurts. It's like—"

"It doesn't hurt me," he said, and then he quoted his favorite artist. "And just because they say the truth hurts, doesn't mean a lie feel good."

In a split second, she went from battered and sobbing to defensive and argumentative. "But you don't have feelings! Remember? How would you know how a lie feels?"

"You're missing the point, and for that reason, among others, I know I could not continue to be involved with you. Get out my house, and have a good life."

He took his keys away from her, though he knew she might have made copies. He'd have to change the locks. And the keys weren't the only thing he took from Katherine that day.

He sat thinking about Katherine's situation and how her self-esteem was lowered because the actions of her boyfriend, but the hold he had over her mentally kept her coming back. Thoughts raced through his mind about how most people in society would not understand Katherine's situation and would tell her, "There's no reason for cheating either. Leave or be faithful." That was easier said than done. He didn't fault Katherine for cheating on her boyfriend with him at all. He understood her situation and the hold her boyfriend had on her. He actually felt the cheating was justified. He would soon go through a series of situations where he felt there was justification.

The first would begin with a private call.

# Chapter 10 Bag of Tricks

## (Danielle)

"Hi, may I speak to Marques?"

"This is me. Who's this?" he asked.

"Melissa reminded me to give you a call. It's Danielle—Danielle Johnson from school. You gave me your number at the grocery store when you were with your girlfriend. Sorry for calling this late. You're not busy are you?"

"Oh. What's up? I'm not busy. Yes, I remember you, and that's not my girlfriend." He chuckled.

"She looked like your girlfriend."

"No. You look like my girlfriend."

"Impossible. I'm married, and you're too young for me anyway."

Seeing that Danielle left room for flirting, Marques continue. "I've been with women much older than you. You're too young for me. And married? Ha! How long have you had that problem?"

"Oh, please. And it's not a problem. How long have you had the problem of not claiming your girlfriend?"

Marques laughed out loud. "She's not my girlfriend. She has a boyfriend. We just had sex until she started acting crazy."

"You probably made her crazy. And why are you trying to break up happy homes?"

"No, I think she's been crazy and just decided to reveal it after we had sex. And that home was far from happy, but that's neither here nor there. Plus, I don't break up happy homes; I make them happier."

"Exactly. Your sex probably made her crazy. And you make them happier? How so?" Danielle had been under pressure from her best friend to cheat on her husband as of late.

"I provide females with laughs, smiles, and no headaches whenever her man isn't acting right. You'll never argue or have a bad time with me, because we wouldn't have time or feelings for that. It's your man's job to make you mad and my job to make it up, and once he notices and feels you disconnecting and getting happiness from somewhere —and trust me, he will notice—if he truly loves you, he'll change his approach and try to win you over all over again."

"Wait. So, let me get this understood. You don't mind being the second option?"

"No. Not at all. It's actually perfect for me. I'm not the relationship type, so the little time where I fill in for your man is fine with me. It means fewer headaches. He gets the headaches, and I get to make it up."

"Wow. I never heard that before."

"Yeah, well you never really held a conversation with me before either."

"Oh, yeah. Thanks for reminding me, because you got me all off my reason for calling. I called to let you know I won't be needing you for the boys and girls club."

"Aw. So you just kicked me to the side, huh? Melissa convinced you to do that, didn't she?" Marques chuckled.

"No! I'm not doing it anymore. My husband wants me to stay home and take care of the house. She actually wouldn't stop rambling about you. She seems obsessed. Did you guys have sex?"

"That's confidential information. I'm not the kind of guy to kiss and tell."

"That's good that you don't."

"It's getting late. You better make sure you have that house taken care of before your husband gets home."

"Oh, be quiet. He won't be here anytime soon. He's too busy taking care of work while I'm left here to take care of the house and myself."

"Yourself? You masturbate?"

"That's confidential information. I'm not the kind of girl to kiss and tell."

Marques could feel her smile through the phone. "Real funny, but no, it's nothing to be ashamed of. I feel all women should masturbate so they can know their bodies and what pleases them."

"Oh, trust me, I know my body. I've only had three sex partners, and besides my husband, I'm the only person who's ever been able to make me cum."

"Oh, so you do. Fingers or toys?"

"Both. When my fingers get tired, I use my bullet."

"Aw, OK. What does he think about you having a bullet?"

"He don't know. He'd probably call me a creep, so I keep the bag of toys in the laundry room. I know he'll never go in there. But speaking of that, it's almost time for me to go get my bag of tricks, so I'll have to talk to you tomorrow."

"OK, good night," said Marques.

Over the next month, the private calls became as frequent as they could get. He talked on the phone with Danielle so much that it was almost like she lived by herself.

Her husband was so dedicated to his job and confident that he had her that he would leave the house for twelve or fourteen hours some days, leaving her ample time to talk to Marques until it was time for her to get her bag of tricks.

But late one night, Marques broke the tradition. He decided to cut her off in the middle of their conversation. "Go get your bag of tricks."

"Why? You're ready to get off the phone with me?"

"No. Just go get them."

"OK, hold on." She put the phone down and head to the laundry room. She was back a minute later with her bag of sex toys." OK, I got them. Now what?"

"Pull your bullet out," he demanded.

"I got it. I just put new batteries in. Want to hear how loud it vibrates?" She turned the bullet on.

"I want to hear how loud you are," said Marques. "Keep one hand on the phone and place the other one on your clit with the bullet."

"OK," she said, arousal in her voice. She lay back and closed her eyes with his seductive voice in her ear. In their fantasy, he rubbed her clit rapidly as he inserted his tongue and licked around the lips of her vagina. He then raised up and started to alternate between biting her neck and sucking her breasts. As he went deeper, and his erection grew, her moans got louder.

"It feels so good, Danielle," he whispered. He picked up the pace. The faster he went, the louder she got. Finally she screamed, "I'm cumming!" Then, quickly, she said, "I have to call you right back."

As Danielle clean herself and the mess she'd made, she thought about how Marques was just able to make her have an orgasm as if she was really having sex with him. And he did it simply by giving her instructions to place the bullet on her clit and insert only one finger in her vagina but not go deep, as if it was a tease. All the while, he made noises like he was eating her out. Then he had her put her legs back and rub her breast before returning her hand to her vagina, this time inserting two fingers and going deeper as he whisper, "It feels so good, Danielle!" And when he notice her moan getting louder, he told her to increase the bullet setting one level at a time, finally hitting the highest, so that it felt like he picked up the pace as she got closer and closer to cumming. She was relieved and ready to sleep now, but not before she calls him back and said, "Thank you, Marques."

He seemed to have her hooked like a fish after the experience. There wasn't a day that went by that she didn't call to end her night with one of their special connections. Marques had introduced her to a whole new world, and he knew it. It had gotten to the point at which she'd do anything he said. His unheard of demands made her adrenaline pump. He had never physically had sex with her. There wasn't even a question of if they would be together on a relationship level, yet she still found herself following his demand of not cheating on him with her husband. He had told her she couldn't have sex with her husband because it would be cheating on him, since he now owned her vagina. Before every phone sex session, she would have to assure him that she wasn't cheating before he would make her cum.

"I promise I didn't cheat on you Marques," she'd say. "I fixed him his dinner plate, told him I was tired and went to sleep early."

# Chapter 11 You're Welcome

## (Danielle Part 2)

After a while, Danielle had a couple of demands of her own. "But, hey, I need you to promise me a couple of things," she said, taking their conversation to a slightly more serious level than they were used to. "One, I need you to promise me that you won't do anything to break my marriage up. I still love my husband dearly, despite his neglecting to spend time with me. I couldn't imagine being without him. Our bond is great, but we're just suffering a disconnection right now. And two, I want you to promise me that you're not all talk—that you can and will make me cum as hard as you do in our phone sessions when we finally do it in person, because I'm well overdue for it. Not cheating on you is really taking a toll on me and my horniness."

Marques laughed. "I normally don't make promises, because it's impossible to foresee situations, but I'm confident in my abilities and definitely aim to please. I'm always on target with that, so I can guarantee you I'm not all talk, and you'll most certainly be pleased. As far as the first one, I can say this again. I'm not setting out to break up your marriage. I make them happier, remember? But I can't control what you do and feel after having sex with me."

"Oh, please. You're so full of yourself. You better be great!" Then Danielle gave him instructions on when and where he could pick her up on the upcoming Friday night when her husband went out with his friends.

"OK, cool, but what if your husband comes home early, notices you're not there, and asks where've you been?"

She already had her lie planned out. "I'll just tell him I was with a friend that I recently started back talking to and haven't seen in years. We decided to go out and have drinks." She'd planned the lie better than they planned their Friday adventure, because on that night it seemed like everything that could go wrong, did.

After Danielle's plan for Marques to pick her up from her friend's house fell through, she decided to just have him come get her from her home, since her husband was gone, or so she thought.

As the time approached, she called Marques. "Hey, where are you?"

"I'm a block away from your street. I should be pulling up within the next two minutes."

"OK! I'm looking out the front window to see if I see you when you pull—wait! No! Keep driving. That's my husband getting out that car right there. I'll call you right back."

As she scramble to get undressed before her husband walk in, Marques rode around the unfamiliar neighborhood. Eventually he parked a few blocks down from her street and waited for her to call back. Ten minutes passed, and there was no call, so he decided to pull off and head home. He only made it a block before finally receiving the call.

"Hey, where are you?" she whispered. "Don't leave. He's in the shower. He just wants me to iron his shirt before he goes out."

"OK, I'm waiting. How turned on are you?" Marques asked.

"Very! But you'll see for yourself shortly. I have to go."

It was another twenty minutes before she was in the clear and in the car with Marques. "My adrenaline is pumping," she said. "I was almost caught. I swear you better be great!"

Marques was nothing less than that once they got back to his apartment. She erupted as soon as he entered her, and she reacted in a way that not even he had witnessed before, making his confidence and erection grow extremely larger with every movement. She orgasmed again and again as she clawed into his back and started shaking like an earthquake—off the Richter scale. He would soon make her reach her climax pinnacle, leaving her all drained out and relaxed to the point at which all she could do was look over, smile at him, and shake her head. She was beyond pleased, but she wasn't the only one. The combination of the warmth and grip of her vagina perfectly fitted to his penis mixed with her passion and ability to lose herself, built his confidence even more. Her reactions during sex made her the best he'd ever had up until that point.

Soon after, Danielle realized that Marques wasn't the only one who couldn't control what she did after they had sex. She couldn't control herself. It was like he had introduced her to a carefree world. She grew more and more nonchalant around her husband. It got to the point at which she was almost never home. She would lie to him and say she was going over her best friend's or her mom's or the club, all just to be with Marques. She grew scared of what she had become, scared for her marriage, scared for her future. She was unstable but figured she could count on her husband being too wrapped up in work to notice. Marques assured her that this wouldn't always be the case.

"If you want to continue seeing me and keep your marriage going, you're going to have to slow down with the visits. Otherwise, your husband is going to notice and grow suspicious."

"Oh, please! He's too caught up in work to notice anything," she said.

"If he loves you and fears losing you, he's definitely going to notice, and you'll notice as soon as he does. Believe it or not, men have intuition too."

"Male intuition? Ha! You clearly don't know my husband. How would I know if he's suspicious of anything, Mr. Know-it-all?" She laugh, but then she attentively waited for his response.

"Laugh all you want, but it's true. If he truly loves you, he'll start seeing the pattern in your actions and change his. He'll feel he's lost you, and he'll start doing things to win you back."

"I doubt it, but I hope you're right. I just want him to get it together. It's almost like I don't exist to him. Why can't he look at me like you do? Why can't I have conversations with him like I do with you?"

"Simple. He's not me. You were seemingly happy with the way he did those things until you met me."

"Yeah, I was. So it's your fault I'm having these thoughts. For your sake, I hope he does get it together."

"For my sake?" said Marques, laughing. "You're crazy, but don't worry, he will."

"OK, I trust you, but I'm not stopping my visits anytime soon."

Danielle's phone chimed with a text from her husband. It said, "Hey, let's go to the art museum tomorrow. I've planned the whole weekend out for us."

Marques looked at her with an I-told-you-so expression on his face, as if he could read her mind. "What does it say?" he asked.

"He wants to go to the art museum tomorrow. I'm going to tell him no."

"What? Why?"

"I don't know. I guess he wants to see the exhibits."

"No, sweetheart, I'm asking why you want to tell him no. We just had a conversation about him noticing and getting it together, and now you want to shoot down his plans?"

"Yeah, I already had my mind set on coming to see you tomorrow, and I don't like the idea of him only noticing because I'm sleeping with you. Why do I have to cheat in order for him to want to make plans with me for the weekend?"

"Who cares? You're not seeing me tomorrow. You're going to go to the museum, and you're going to enjoy it."

"Why?" she asked. "Why do you care if I go with him or not?"

"I don't care. I told you I would make your home happier, and I'm just a man of my word."

A man of his word and a man who knew he wasn't ready or willing to provide a home, happy or not, for Danielle or anyone else at the moment.

The blocked phone calls began to occur less and less as the days and weeks went by, the last and final one being one that Marques knew all so well, but this time it was for a different reason.

"Thank you, Marques," Danielle said as she smiled through the phone.

"You're welcome," he said before ending the call. Even though Danielle cheated with him, he admired how she didn't want him to break up her relationship. It wouldn't be long before Marques would end up involved with another female who was in a relationship.

# Chapter 12 Payback: Enough is Enough

## (Patrice)

This time it was Patrice, a high maintenance college girl he had met in the same department store as Katherine. And much like Katherine, she turned down his advances because of her relationship status. She had been with the same guy for little over five years and couldn't see herself entertaining another guy's attention, let alone cheating. Marques acknowledged and respected her loyalty to her boyfriend, and he befriended her. He would occasionally text her to see if she was all right. He let her vent to him in situations like when her grandmother passed and, more recently, with the secret about her boyfriend that she'd been keeping and that had been eating her up inside.

She was reluctant to tell him at first, out of fear that he would use it to manipulate her.

Marques, seeing that, reassured her that wasn't his aim. He told her she could always count on him. "Go ahead, vent. Just let it flow."

And that's exactly what she did. She told him how she had caught her boyfriend of five years cheating with his "platonic" female friend. She had always suspected but didn't believe it till she saw it herself. She had come in contact with the other woman, who'd told her everything, from the little pet names he called her to the unprotected sex with they had. Patrice couldn't believe how she had let him pull wool over her eyes. She was blinded by love, her own stubbornness, and pride. It was the same pride that wouldn't allow her to leave him for fear that her mother and father, who adored and respected her boyfriend, would look at her like a failure. So she told no one but a nonjudgmental and understanding Marques. And even though she was reluctant to tell him at first because he might take advantage of her weakened state, that's exactly what she wanted him to do. She wanted revenge. She wanted to get even with her boyfriend.

Seeing so, Marques tried to give her other outs before going back on his word of not manipulating her. "I can't really give my take on this, because I don't know his side of the story. You seem like a pretty decent girlfriend. Why would he cheat? How do you know she wasn't lying?"

"I'm a great girlfriend. I don't know why he would cheat. But I believed her because her days matched up. She described how his sex was good but selfish and lazy, and I definitely know my man. Plus, I always suspected it. My woman's intuition wouldn't steer me wrong."

"Oh! Well you seem pretty set, so why not try your ex?" asked Marques.

"He's too clingy. He'll start buying me too many gifts which wouldn't be bad, since my boyfriend has slowed down in that department, but that would push my guy away and I want my relationship. I don't want to move on. I've invested five years. He's the only guy my parents have ever accepted, and if I go back for revenge sex with my ex, he'll think it's more than it really is and try to ruin my relationship."

"Oh, I understand, Tricey Boo," he said with a smirk on his face.

"Boo?" she asked with a smile. "Well, Boo, come here and help me take my bra off so I can get comfortable. Don't try anything funny," she warned him before bending over in front of him, revealing she didn't have any underwear on under her skirt. He began to fondle her. He reached for a condom, but then decided not to use it.

As soon as he entered her, she screamed, "Yes!" He was fulfilling her every need to feel revenge. The calling of a pet name, unprotected sex, and though her boyfriend's sex was good, Marques was going above and beyond to show her what non lazy sex feels like. And on top of that, it was happening with a guy who was her platonic friend. She was pleased. Her legs were shaking, juices were dripping, her face was glowing, and her heart was pounding. But right along with that, her mind was racing, and her conscience kicked in. This wasn't her.

"We have to stop!" she said.

Marques slowly pulled back out of her. She had an ashamed look on her face. She couldn't believe how low she'd just stooped to get back at her boyfriend. She threw all her morals and beliefs out the window. But her pride was a little heavier than those feelings, and that made it hard to throw it out or even move it to the side. Pride is what led to her back over and over. But along with her pride came her conscience.

"We have to stop! Why are you steady taking advantage of me?" she asked.

"Taking advantage? I'm letting you use me and helping get your relationship back on track," Marques explained.

"How is seducing me and taking advantage of my vulnerability helping my relationship get back on track? All you're doing is confusing me more."

Marques counted off the points. "One, stop saying I'm taking advantage of you. I'm only giving you what you want and need. Two, stick with me long enough, and that intuition you're always raving about? You'll find that men have it too. And once your guy sees you drifting, he'll step his game up."

"I hope you're right, but what if he doesn't?" she asked hopelessly

"He will, but if you're impatient, you step yours up. Make him feel there's no reason to go be with another woman. From experience, I know that things tend to fade after being in a relationship for so long. Rekindle that flame."

"From experience? But you've never been in a relationship before."

"No, I haven't, but I've been with a couple of women who were. Trust me. Do you perform oral sex on him?"

"No," said Patrice. "That stopped when my gifts slowed down."

"Oh! Well do this: Call him up and tell him you all need to talk. Ask if you can come over. When you get there, tell him to come outside to your car. Once he's in the car, just start kissing him, and work your way down. Please him."

She listened, and in came the gifts and attention. Patrice's relationship was back on track, and Marques had once again helped a female he saw potential in make it right with another guy.

After the very similar episodes with Danielle and Patrice, what once seemed a challenge of pleasing and helping females in relationships had become rather easy, due to how much their men had neglected the relationships. Those men soon regretted it, once it became clear that they could lose their women. The two were practically pushed into his bed and yanked out. Marques grew tired of it and decided he needed more. He needed a challenge, something of his own. He needed a girlfriend. He thought about it for several days. Loraine had moved back to the city. Marques made several advances toward her, which she rejected, but they settled into being friends. So Marques discussed his new ideas with her, and she agreed. So it was set. He was getting a girlfriend. But who? Who was worthy and still presented a challenge? Who could he put even the smallest amount of trust in and receive trust from her? He sat deep in thought on who it should be. He even mapped out the criteria he was looking for in a girlfriend in his head. He would go on to deal with numerous females while Loraine observed how he treated the women. She often warned him, "You can't keep leading these females on like this. Karma's going to get you. I can't wait until you finally find a girlfriend she's going to be hell on you."

"I hope you're right. Then I'll have a challenge," said Marques, who continued to scout out the different females. Almost all seemed to want to change him, and there were many of them.

# Chapter 13
## Foresee...It could never Work out

There were the ones like Annie and Kenya, who had no connection past sexual with him and were only using him for a temporary fix until their guys got back on track. Then there were the girls like Queenie and Whitney, who would claim they couldn't have sex with him right away, because it was an act only done by "whores." But they were easily seduced into sexual activities with him. Marques couldn't help but think that since they did what they thought only whores did, they considered themselves whores. He went on to tell them that, due to the fact they were quick to judge and even quicker to have their minds changed, a relationship with him could never work out.

And then there were girls like Ciara and a few others, who had the characteristics he was looking for in a girlfriend, but who were so broken and skeptical from prior relationships that they didn't even bother to try and change him. They just took it for what is was and indulged in sex and conversation with him. Even if feelings had developed, they were afraid to show him, given their pasts and what they knew about him. But sooner than later the feelings would overshadow what they knew, and they would eventually try to make it more. But Marques knew that them knowing about his past would only lead to them being too insecure, so he'd let them know it could never work out.

Then there were the females he admired and found very attractive, but who he couldn't quite grasp mentally, like Lisa and others. He'd occasionally have great sex with them, but only at their convenience, because they were into living their lives and only needed a guy for sex when they wanted it. His controlling ways conflicted with that, so he let them know, after a last intense round of sex, that it could never work out.

Then there were the females whose stories really intrigued him. But because he knew their stories, he would subconsciously use them. Kim and Mya fit into this category. Kim was an aspiring model who was stranded and lost when Marques met her, but he could see she was lost in more ways than one. She immediately opened up to him about being raped by her uncle when she was just eleven years old. She felt like her innocence was robbed from her, and she had become a woman at that very moment. Pleasing her sexually and mentally by making her feel wanted and protected, Marques soon had her attached to him, but it wasn't long before he distanced himself from her. After two sessions of sex, Kim pitched the idea of having unprotected sex. Marques was totally against the idea, especially since she talked about how she thought the two would make a beautiful baby girl. It seemed to him that she was trying to get back the innocence that was robbed from her by having a child. He totally understood, but he couldn't allow himself to assist with it, given the fact he had no connection with her outside of sex. For that reason, he let her know that it could never work out.

Then there was females like Mya, who had a body like a stallion and immediately developed a sexual connection with Marques. But she said she couldn't engage in any sexual activities with him, because she was engaged to get married soon. She went on and opened up to him with a story similar to Kim's. She too had been sexually abused as a child. Only difference was, this time it was by one of the many guys her mom had in and out of their home to fulfill her loneliness. She told him that she'd always had a body that would make her appeal to older guys. That's what drew her mother's friend into raping her on late nights. She stressed how she didn't want to use it as an excuse to be promiscuous, but she definitely felt it played a part. Her vulnerability made it easy for Marques to make her forget about being engaged and have sex with him. Then he looked past her physical makeup and ability to be honest and decide she was too broken. He let her know immediately following their second session of sex that it could never work out.

Then there were females like Hilary, who reminded him of past situations. Hilary was much like Mya's mom. She was lonely and subjected her two-year-old son to being around different guys just so she could fulfill her loneliness.

Marques couldn't help but think about Mya and Kim's situations one night at Hilary's place. She had left the bedroom door open a crack so she could hear her son if he woke up. But she didn't hear him that night until he pushed the door open and saw Marques having sex with his mother. It disgusted Marques. He thought about how many other guys this might have happened with and how many guys like Kim's uncle or Mya's abuser she might have exposed her son to. Her not putting her son's safety over her personal needs let Marques know exactly what his text to her should say. And he let her know that it could never work out.

Then there were females from past situations who emerged, like Patrice. She was now single. Her boyfriend had broken up with her because her trust issues and the false accusations she frequently made when she thought about how he had cheated on her before.

She vented to Marques. "We had a disconnect. I can't talk to him like I can you. I can't trust him like I can you." She had trust issues, and her trust issues made her insecure and unstable. So Marques told her they could never be together.

Then there were the females who were career oriented, like Italia. She was a psychology major at CSU. She and Marques would often have deep conversations, sometimes debates, about human functions. One day this lead to a talk about a woman's ability to have multiple orgasms. Italia had taken a class in which she learned of studies that said it was rare for women to have multiple orgasms. Marques knew then that they wouldn't be able to go forward. With his desire to please women and her mind believing she couldn't be pleased in such a way, them having sex was pointless, although he did give it one shot before telling her that they could never work out.

Then there were the girls who had tons of potential but met Marques at the wrong time in life, like Brooklyn. She was a young, innocent-looking girl who seemed mature beyond her age. She seemed troubled by something when Marques met her downing shots of liquor while she was under medication at a party they both attended. Marques was instantly drawn to her. He wanted to know her story. Her looks didn't hurt either. They exchanged numbers, and Marques found out what weighed on her mind. Brooklyn had so many high expectations put on her by her family due to the failures of her older sibling. It was overwhelming for her at times, but she dealt with it, and Marques was intrigued by her being able to do so. The two traded ideas about life, among other things, before having sex. The sex was very intense, and Marques took a dominant role at Brooklyn's request. It turned her on, but not as much as her pleasing him did. She would do anything to please him. She was almost perfect in his eyes, except for one thing: she still had those expectations weighing on her, and he didn't want to get in the way her ambitions, so he told her, "You're going to make some guy a perfect wife one day, but we could never work out."

Then there was Mariah. She had the prettiest, most innocent face ever. She was gorgeous. She was born on March 23, making her an Aries. Marques wasn't completely into astrology, but it had been said that Aries and Gemini had a high compatibility. Mariah was a bit nonchalant and had the ability to hide her feelings with an amazing smile and big beautiful eyes. And she was doing just that when Marques met her on the train platform, she was in the wake of a really bad breakup, but you wouldn't know it, because she was able to smile her way through it. Marques only found out through her being honest on one of the many nights they sat and talked on the phone for hours. She was just like him in some ways and very different from him in even more. She was a partygoer who loved dancing and was very social. He was so drawn to her that they hit it off immediately, telling stories to one another about their pasts. And although it was only a month by the time they first had sex, there was so much chemistry between them that their bodies were totally in sync with each other. It was amazing. They went on for about eight months as just sex partners.

Then Mariah did what seemed to be almost impossible: she made Marques feel. She made him feel angry when he heard that she'd mentioned him as someone she only liked and hung out with while putting forth an effort to mend things with her ex. He felt that she should've just left his name out. So Marques stepped out of character and had an argument with her before telling her they could never workout.

Then there were girls like Michelle. She and Marques had mutual friends who fixed them up. Michelle seemed to want to immediately rush into a relationship with Marques. After they met, she wanted to make it official with him and introduce him to her family right away. But there were a few problems. First, Marques didn't want to rush into a relationship, especially since he didn't know her and was still weighing his options. Second, she had a crazy rule about waiting five months before they had sex, which was absurd to someone like Marques. He felt sex was a part of nature and not something you plan to have or put a time frame on having. Plus, sex would play a major part in any relationship he decided to be in, so he would need to know right away how good his partner was. And third, the more he talked to her and came around, the more obvious it became that she was simply trying to escape the abusive relationship with her child's father. He beat her small frame like she was a heavyweight boxer. Marques viewed it as a repeat of Katherine's situation, and he didn't want any part of it, so after he seduced her into having sex with him four months before she originally planned, he called her and told her, "We could never work out. I just got into a relationship."

*Chapter 13 Challenges and Tattoos*

Eventually, Marques chose who he wanted to be in a relationship with. She was naturally beautiful and possessed some of the same characteristics he did. She was witty, charismatic, and had an extremely high sex drive. And although he would never get a tattoo, she sported some that were exactly the ones he would get if he ever decided to do that. One said, "Loyalty." Another said, "Respect." One proclaimed, "Fearless." Another said, "What lies within." There was another that said, "My brother's keeper." A rather large one on her back described him to a tee. She also possessed traits that Marques couldn't even begin to think about having. She was caring, friendly, and very sociable. She gave off a vibe that made people automatically take to her and love her. Marques would normally have to use his charisma and wits to win people over. He admired her qualities. What he admired even more was her ability to genuinely care for another person's feelings. Outside of family, he had never cared for someone. He found it amazing that she was able to genuinely do so. Those things made her worthy. The thing that made her a challenge in his eyes was her possessiveness. He figured that him being nonchalant and her being possessive would clash. And there was also the fact that she'd been raised in a household with her father. That was decades of another man's thoughts and beliefs being programmed into her, along with her being genuinely loved by a man. So there wasn't much Marques would be able to get by her, and it would be rather hard for him to instill his beliefs in her. He knew Mariah was the one.

They reunited just before Marques's birthday. Mariah had been betrayed by her boyfriend in a way that cut her deep. She was extremely hurt but, somehow, still remembered Marques's birthday and reached out to him to bring him a gift. She was hesitant at first about reaching out, given the way they'd left off, but she was assured all was forgiven. And when the conversation about getting into a relationship was brought up, she assured him that, unlike everyone else, she didn't want to change him. She wanted him to remain the same. He appreciated that and the only gift he'd receive from someone other than his mother since his grandmother had passed.

He assured her of something that she found rather odd but definitely appreciated. "I understand that you were with your boyfriend for years. I understand that you had a bond. I understand that you love him, and despite what he's done to you, you won't just be able to turn those feelings off overnight. I understand all these things, and I still want to be with you. I know it'll take some time, but I'm willing to take that time with you and help you get over him. Just don't lie to me, and try to be as understanding as I am. That's all I ask."

She said, "OK. I really appreciate you acknowledging that. I will never lie to you, and I'm confident that the love I have for him won't be able to compare to the love we'll have for each other."

"You think you can get me to love?" he asked in a sarcastic manner, and he laughed.

"Yes. I do, and I will," she said confidently. And she did just that after months of bonding, pushing each other to their limits, balancing each other out, and Mariah consistently telling and showing Marques she loved him. He was doing things he'd never in a million years think he would be doing, from surprising her with jewelry he bought at Tiffany's just because, to taking her on picnics in millennium park and bike riding alongside the lake. He gave her get-well-soon cards when she had headaches. He watched her blush and saw her eyes light up like the sky at Navy Pier on their Fourth of July date when he finally said, "I love you."

He had felt something he had never felt before. He genuinely loved her and cared for her. And so did everyone around him—his mom, his friends, even Loraine and the females he used to have sex with, who occasionally called for advice. They all seemed to love her. She and Marques had developed a storybook kind of bond, they naturally balanced each other when together, finishing each other's sentences. She even began to talk like him. Their bond was amazing. She wanted to do nothing but be around him at all times. She had distanced herself from old friends and stopped partying all together. She catered to his every need and supported every idea and business venture he had, and there were plenty. She even supported the latest one, which seemed to consume a lot of Marques's time and created a disconnect, causing her to share his attention, which she normally wanted all of.

"Hey, baby, can you put that on hold for the day so we can go out?" she asked.

"No, love, I need to get this done," he said. "I feel it. This is the one that's going to have us comfortable for the rest of our lives."

"OK, baby, be great. I'll just go home, call Ariel, and go out with her tonight," she said as she pouted.

Stopping what he was doing, he looked up and asked, "Who's Ariel?"

"Ariel. Ariel's the girl that I'm always with. You know Ariel, my friend since grammar school. I saw her recently and told her we could go out for drinks if you and I weren't doing anything."

"Oh, OK, baby. Have fun and enjoy yourself. Let me know when you make it home safe. I love you."

"I love you more," she said before receiving a kiss on both cheeks and her forehead.

The disconnect continued, but it wasn't so much about not having time. It was more so about Loraine. Mariah didn't like the bond Marques and Loraine had. She didn't like how it seemed unbreakable and how Loraine appeared to want Marques as more than a friend.

"Why does she always have to be around?" Mariah said. "Why does she text and call you for advice?" Then she answered her own question. "She likes you. I can tell. She wants to be with you, and I don't like it. You guys can't be friends anymore. Tell her to never contact you again."

He replied in a calm voice. "No. That's stupid. What difference does it make if she wants me if I don't want her? What? You don't trust me?"

"No. It's not that I don't trust you. I don't trust women. I know how they can be, and I'm selfish. I don't want to be sharing you. I'm a bit intimidated by her."

"Shut up. That's stupid. Why would you be intimidated by her when you have what she allegedly wants and look much better than her? She always says how pretty you are."

"Don't call me stupid, Marques," she yelled

"One, I didn't call you stupid. I would never do that. And two, lower your voice when talking to me," he said in the calmest voice.

"I'm sorry, baby. I apologize. Let's just have sex. I don't want to argue anymore." She looked at him with puppy dogs eyes.

Now, while Marques didn't feel they were arguing or anything had gotten resolved, he didn't mind ending it all to have sex. And why shouldn't he? She had become the best he'd ever had. She was so in tune with her body that she was almost naturally stimulated. Adding that to her mental, emotional, and physical attraction to him made it beyond easy for him to please her repeatedly. He made her feel as if she was having an out-of-body experience every time. It was amazing how well they connected. It was like a whole other level than either of them had experienced before. It had also served as a way for them to forget the past. And forgetting the past was something they were big on. They both knew of each other's pasts and didn't care to judge one another on them but rather help each other forget about them. They called it the Purple Heart effect, named after the Purple Heart medal awarded to those wounded or killed in action. And while they wouldn't dare feel they could compare their past hurtful issues in life with the sacrifices of the brave souls who'd gone to battle for our country, they did feel that they were both wounded in the past and rewarded with each other. As the months went by, the disconnect seemed to disappear, and they grew stronger.

Mariah, so excited about the growth, didn't want to waste any time in taking the next step. "Hey, what do you think about us moving in together?" she asked one day.

"I don't think we're ready," he said without hesitation.

"Why not? Explain!"

"I think that's a big step. Like how would we split rent? Who pays what bills? When you bring finances into a relationship, it turns more into a business partnership, and we haven't discussed taking that step yet."

Showing her upbringing, Mariah said, "Well, that's easy. My Dad always told me, 'It's the man's job to provide the home for the family.' So that leaves rent to you. And he said, 'It's the woman's job to take care of the home.' So there you have it. Once I move in, that'll be the first step to getting married and having children. Well, I'm not sure about the children side of it just yet."

"I'm sure we're not ready for that. I love you and wouldn't want to rush something that could potentially ruin our relationship. You suffer from Daddy's-little-girl syndrome. I respect your father and admire your relationship with him, but that's not how I see things. As far as marriage goes, I guess I can do it, if it's what you want. You know I'm not too much into titles. As for the children side of it, Ha! You wouldn't dare want to split my attention with someone else."

"Did you just call me a spoiled, attention-seeking brat?" she asked. "How long have you been holding that in?"

"Not as long as I've been holding these," he said with a smile. Then he reached into his pocket and withdrew a pair of beautiful 14 karat gold hoop earrings.

Mariah was in awe, not only because of how beautiful the earrings were, but because she had told Marques she wanted some gold hoop earrings during one of the periods when he seemed too focused on his project.

"So you were listening?" she asked.

"Yeah, I always listen to you, baby. Listen, not hear."

"Well, listen to me when I say this. I want to spend some time with you tonight. Put the project aside, and let's do something."

"OK, cool," he said. "I'll make reservations. Get dressed. Wear a dress and heels!"

Marques took her to an upscale restaurant, where he ordered for her and they joked, laughed and seemed more in love than ever. It would continue through the night as they walked through the well-lit, beautiful city and enjoyed each other's company. Then they went to the 24-hour convenient store and picked up movies and snacks.

They only made it halfway through the first movie before they were all over each other. This had become the norm. Marques put his project off for a while and became fully focused on pleasing Mariah and giving her his time. They were inseparable until Mariah birthday was approaching. She instantly went back to her old party-girl self.

"Hey, baby, I haven't been out in a while," she said with excitement. "I'm going to go out for my birthday month!"

Marques laughed. "Oh, would you look at that? Most people only get a birthday. Not you, though. You get a whole month!"

"Don't be an asshole, Marques. It's just that I haven't been out in a while, and I miss it."

"Go ahead. Enjoy yourself. I'm catering to you the day and weekend of your birthday, though, so the club can't have you those days," he replied, not knowing the club would have her for more than the days of her birthday month. It was like she was a drug addict, and the club was her fix. She began going two and three times a week, sometimes four. She felt it was all right as long as she ended the night with Marques, who had started back working on his project. She'd come in from the club and demand he put his work to the side so they could have sex and spend time together.

"No, I really need to get this done," he said. "I've been putting it off too long. You want to spend more time together, manage your club-going time better."

"You have a problem with me going out, Marques?" she asked.

"No, but if it's effecting our time together, then yeah. I mean, you do go out an awful lot."

"OK, I won't go out, but you have to cut back on some time-consuming things too."

"Time-consuming things like what, Mariah?"

"This project you're doing involving these whores—texting and talking to the whore, Loraine, Marques!"

"Being a whore is in the eye of the beholder," he said. "You can't judge people."

"Are you taking up for them whores?" She asked.

"You missed the point!" Marques realized she'd also missed the point about not going out so much to give them more time together. She viewed it as if he was just saying it because he didn't like her going out. So she began to ask before she went now.

"Hey, baby, what are you doing?" she asked over the phone one night. "Can I go out tonight?"

"Don't ask me that," He demanded.

"Whoa! I can't ask what you're doing?"

"Let's not be assholes, Mariah. I'm talking about you asking me to go out. I'm not going to be determining whether you go out or not. If you want to go out, then go."

"OK. I'm going to go, but just because it's Ariel's birthday. This will be the last time I go out for a while."

"Ha! Why don't I believe you?" He asked in a joking manner.

"You probably don't believe anything I say," she said, raising her voice. Before he could reply, she apologized. "You know what? I'm sorry for raising my voice at you. How's your project going?"

"It's going good. I don't want to stop the flow. I'll talk to you later when you come over."

Marques got a visitor later that night, but it wasn't Mariah, it was Loraine. She came over happy and on a mission, and left even happier, feeling like she had accomplished something she'd been trying to do for the longest.

Marques spent the night thinking about everything from the Loraine situation to his future with Mariah, what he was about to say to her when she got there, and what he had become. But Mariah didn't arrive after leaving the club. He didn't hear from her until the next morning when she called on the phone.

"Hello," said Mariah her voice cracking.

"Hello. I was just about to call you," said Marques. "We need to talk."

"No! No we don't," said Mariah, obviously upset. "I'm done talking. You've done me wrong. I've seen it with my own eyes. You've lied to, betrayed, and disrespected me. I don't see how we could go forward."

Not caring to even ask what she's talking about, he said, "Me either. It's over." And he ended the call.

*Chapter 14 No Love Lost, answers found*

*(Mariah Part 2 )*

It had been months since she had spoken to Marques, but that didn't keep her from keeping up with the progress of his project through the promotions he had been putting out. She felt it was cool that he still found a way to include her in the project even though they had broken up. He released it on a very special day to both of them, April 13. She figured she'd support him but, more importantly, see if she could get an explanation for the break up without talking directly to him. She knew he'd probably just make her angry and upset with his nonchalant attitude.

She frantically rushed out to purchase the book and then back home to begin reading. Immediately she saw a situation and phone conversation that she knew too well.

The passage read:

After witnessing what she'd seen and crying herself to sleep, she figured she had enough evidence and been through enough pain to call it quits. She picked up the phone and made the call.

He answered, "Hello. I was just about to call you. We need to talk."

So drained from crying all morning that she couldn't even yell to show her real frustration, she replied in a voice of a person who'd had enough. "No. No we don't. I'm done talking. You've done me wrong. I've seen it with my own eyes. You've lied to, betrayed, and disrespected me. I don't see how we could go forward."

Not caring to even ask what she was talking about, he replied, "Me either. It's over." And he ended the call.

The memories of that day and the breakup instantly made her tear up, but soon after she became furious as she read about his encounters with Loraine. She had always expected the two were more than just platonic friends, and the story of her being his first just confirmed that what she'd seen that night was true. Marques was having an affair with Loraine. Her mind drifted from the book as she reenact the night before the breakup in her head.

It replayed vividly. Loraine walked out of his apartment building with a devious look on her face at four in the morning as Mariah pulled up from her night at the club. Mariah then redirect her focus to the book, only to learn an interesting fact about Marques. Immediately after learning Loraine was his first sex partner, she learned that she wasn't the only one he didn't ejaculate with while having sex. She also learned it had nothing to do with her and that he was pleased by simply pleasing her. She smirked as she read it.

> While in the shower, he smiled to himself, adrenaline still pumping. He realized that even though he didn't ejaculate, he had still gotten off. He was pleased with the fact that he had pleased Loraine and that she wanted there to be a "next time" and that she had to "get ready" for him after feeling his size. Awkwardly the thought of pleasing a woman outweighed the fact that he had just broken his virginity."

That smirk soon turned into a frown as she began reading about how his trust in people was destroyed at a young age due to his father actions, which led her to think about the women-can't-be-trusted conversation he'd had with his mom early on in the book. She started feeling bad for him and began to understand why he never made promises to her.

She got more comfortable as she began to read about Ms. Butler. And she started thinking out loud. "He's the sweetest asshole I've ever met," she said as she read about him turning the prom date with Sharon down. "I would've been mad at her too, canceling on you for a mystery guy."

The commentating continues as she reads on. "I want my 'good father' back. He was perfect. A good father. Humph. Sounds about right. That trifling slut! She cheated on my baby, and he still befriended her after?"

She understood more about the trust issues he had as she read further into the book and saw how Loraine broke their vow and took away what little hope he ever had for trusting a woman. She continued.

"I know he didn't have sex with his teacher."

"Oh, wow, he had sex with his teacher!"

"Oh, wait. No, she was just daydreaming."

"What? So, he did have sex with her!"

"Wait! What? So Loraine was her roommate? Wow!"

"Aw, my poor baby missed his grandma."

"Aw, my poor baby! This inconsiderate bitch raped him while he was mourning *and* she got pregnant?"

"Oh, OK, she didn't get pregnant. She better have been on birth control."

"She's crazy! She's using sex to get out of everything, because she knows he's a sex addict!" She shook her head and continued reading about Melissa taking advantage of Marques being a nympho after she proposed the idea of him moving in and taking care of her bills.

"Don't fall for it, ba—" She stopped mid sentence. She now understood why Marques might've been skeptical about them moving in together at first. His guard was up because of how Melissa tried to take advantage of him. Intrigued by this finding, she read on. She found it very interesting that she could relate to Katherine. She too felt beat up and vulnerable at times. Even though Marques never physically beat her, he often did mentally. When she would constantly go out, he'd make her feel stupid about it, just as he had done with other decisions she made that he didn't approve of. As she read on, she found it even more interesting that she had a similar conversation to the one Katherine had with her boyfriend, which Marques had coached her through.

"Wow! How could he think anything besides that was going on?" she asked herself before drifting off into flashbacks of having sex with Marques and him moaning in her ear in that manly way, just as the book said he'd done with Katherine. She would soon see that her initial thoughts of being able to relate to Katherine were crazy, just as she thought Katherine was.

"Oh, my God! She really stole his keys?"

"Wow, she was really going through it. Maybe I can't relate to her. She's crazy, and Marques never made me feel like I couldn't talk to him."

She felt bad for Katherine, but she couldn't help but smirk as she read how he got rid of her. "Yeah, that's Marques for you. Understanding but unbending, always giving tough love, the sweetest asshole I know."

"It's funny how he was able to figure out Danielle's problem and provide her with time and attention, but he couldn't give me all the time and attention I wanted. Always talking about he's work, if that's what you want to call revisiting your past years with all these sluts."

She began to get irritated again by the fact that he had provided Danielle with two of things that she complained about toward the end of their relationship but didn't receive. She grew past irritated once she read that Danielle was "the best" he'd ever had till that point in his life. She was furious, shaking her head and turning red. "He's going to call this whore, another man's whore, the best he ever had? And to think she was the whore I was beginning to sympathize with the most. Humph!"

"Male intuition? He's living proof that that's not always the case. Marques is too stubborn and nonchalant to have that, his little stupid self being so sure."

She soon began to reminisce about the good times, then she quickly switched back to anger. "The museum? The art museum? Man how I would love to spend another day there with my Marques, but noooo, he wanted to go and be stupid. Who cheats and just breaks up with the person they hurt by cheating? A true asshole."

Eager to find out why he was so quick to break up with her, Mariah skimmed through the rest of the book. Nothing stood out to her, other than all the ups and downs that they appeared to have that went unnoticed by her and how good Marques was at reading her. And the similar situations between her and Patrice, both dealing with a guy with a platonic friend. Before she knew it, she was there. She had made it to what seemed to be leading into the last chapter.

To those of you reading this, you're probably thinking "oh he's really an asshole. How could he break up with her after he was the one cheating on her?" Well easy! I didn't cheat.

Mariah eagerly turned the page to find a big surprise, something she thought was a secret.

*Chapter 15 Womanized?*

*(Marques)*

She did! That's right, she cheated. The night before she called, upset and accusing me, Loraine had come over to show me some pictures she had taken of Mariah and another guy being affectionate with one another in a club earlier that night. Loraine seemed to have left my place satisfied, knowing she had potentially broken up our relationship. She left with the devious smile on her face, advising me to do what's best for me. I began to think about the conversation Mariah and I would have once she came in from the club, but she never arrived. I let my thoughts drift and came to a conclusion.

Even though Mariah cheated on me, I didn't blame her. I mean, it was pretty selfish to expect someone to not go out and seek attention, time, and affection from someone else when you're not providing those things. I was aware that our relationship had reached a point where I no longer gave Mariah those things. I was also aware of why I stopped: Mariah making me love and care for her opened my eyes to what I really was—a womanizer. I mean, everything she did made me think about the women in my past. The moment she brought up having children, all I could think about was the couple of women I'd dealt with who not only were molested and had their childhoods taken away from them by sick-minded, scum-of-the-earth perverts, but were also taken advantage of by me, a guy who saw their situations and subconsciously used them to his advantage. I couldn't imagine bringing a child into this world knowing that there was a chance they might experience that. Oh, and the moving in together situation, when she told me how she was raised and how the man takes care of the household I couldn't help but think of the whole Melissa situation. Speaking of Melissa, I once told her that for a relationship to work, a guy must be like a good father and have balance, which I really believed. That's why Mariah asking me if she could go out let me know we couldn't work. The balance was gone. It had gotten to a point where she viewed me as a strict father the day we had a strikingly similar conversation to the one I coached Katherine through with her boyfriend the first time we had sex. From there on, I began to think about how it was me who pushed her off. Even though I was unaware of what I was doing, it was almost like I followed a playbook on how to make your girlfriend cheat! A playbook I had worked against to get Katherine, Danielle, and Patrice to cheat with me. I had the platonic friend in Loraine, just like Patrice's boyfriend. I began to work so much that I was neglecting her, just like Danielle's husband did her. And while I would never commit the cowardly act of putting my hands on any female in a violent manner, I had beat her mentally, putting a strain on her mind just as Katherine's boyfriend had done to her body. I was inconsiderate of her feelings, not appreciative of her time, and mentally abusive. All that made it hard for her to talk to me. I couldn't help it. It was like she made me see the one thing I didn't have control of, which was my mind. It was almost like I blacked out and just went into scenarios I knew so well. So what else would I expect of her besides reacting just as those women did. So I guess her cheating wasn't really the reason I broke up with her, but her showing me who I really was—that was the main reason. When I look in the mirror, I don't see myself. I see shadows of the women of my past, and all the lessons I learned from and used against them are what make me. But I see Mariah more vividly than anyone. I saw the real me through her. I'm a womanizer. I couldn't help but push her off. I hated seeing it. I hated the fact that she showed me how all these women opened up to me, and I subconsciously used everything I learned from them to get my way with them. More importantly, I hated the fact that all the women I never cared about from my past dictated the outcome of my relationship with the only woman I ever cared about and loved. Like even while writing this book,I found myself rushing through the scenarios with those females and only recalling our sexual encounters and everything that surrounded them. While the focal point of Mariah's portion of the book was how she made me feel. I loved her, I love her but can't be with her because of how she remind me of a past I'm not so proud of. But I can't and won't blame her or them. It's not their fault. They're the victims. They were…

Mariah closed the book slowly and looked at the front cover of the book written by Marques and the title, WOMANIZED.

WOMANIZED
BY Marques Thomas
*Inspired By A True Story*
GREYZONE COMMISSION